CRITICAL THINKING

AND

PROBLEM SOLVING

MEGAN KOPP

Crabtree Publishing Company
www.crabtreebooks.com

Author: Megan Kopp

Series research and development: Reagan Miller

Editors: Rachel Minay, Kathy Middleton, and Janine Deschenes

Proofreader: Kelly Spence

Designer: Rocket Design Ltd

Photo researchers: Megan Kopp and Rachel Minay

Cover design: Katherine Berti

Production coordinator and prepress technician: Tammy McGarr

Print coordinator: Katherine Berti

Produced for Crabtree Publishing by White-Thomson Publishing

Photographs:
Alamy: Joseph Project – Malawi: p. 34, NASA: p. 21b; Shutterstock: 2jenn: p. 7t, Africa Studio: p. 43, Alessia Pierdomenico: p. 31b, alexmillos: p. 11t, Anastasios71: p. 11b, Angela Shvedova: p. 38b, Angela Waye: p. 27t, Anna Omelchenko: p. 41, Ashwin: p. 35, aslysun: p. 6l, biletskiy: pp. 44–45, Billion Photos: p. 36, BortN66: p. 19, Bruce Rolff: p. 26, CRM: p. 39t, Dean Drobot: pp. 6r, 39b, dizain: p. 16, Elena Elisseeva: p. 14, Iconic Bestiary: p. 22t, iQoncept: p. 17, Kuliperko: p. 18, Lightspring: p. 31t, Lyudmyla Kharlamova: p. 8, Malchev: p. 12, Mammut Vision: p. 27b, Michael D Brown: p. 30, michaeljung: p. 42, Monkey Business Images: pp. 13, 40, MR.LIGHTMAN1975: p. 9, nanami7: p. 4, Orla: p. 33, Pablo Scapinachis: p. 29, Ovidiu Hrubaru: p. 44, pathdoc: p. 5, Piotr Marcinski: p. 6c, plavevski: p. 38t, Rauf Aliyev: p. 5, Rawpixel.com: pp. 22–23, Reno Martin: p. 25, Ron Ellis: p. 7t, sixninepixels: p. 28, snvv: pp. 32–33, suphakit73: p. 15, Syda Productions: p. 10, Vitezslav Valka: p. 20, VLADGRIN: pp. 14, 24t, whiteisthecolor: p. 21t; Stefan Chabluk: p. 24b.

All other images by Shutterstock

Library and Archives Canada Cataloguing in Publication

Kopp, Megan, author
        Above and beyond with critical thinking and problem solving / Megan Kopp.

(Fueling your future! going above and beyond in the 21st century)
Includes index.
Issued in print and electronic formats.
ISBN 978-0-7787-2842-9 (hardback).--
ISBN 978-0-7787-2846-7 (paperback).--
ISBN 978-1-4271-1836-3 (html)

        1. Critical thinking--Juvenile literature. 2. Decision making--Juvenile literature. 3. Problem solving--Juvenile literature. I. Title.

BF441.K677 2016   j153.4   C2016-903311-2
                                     C2016-903312-0

Library of Congress Cataloging-in-Publication Data

CIP available at the Library of Congress

Crabtree Publishing Company
www.crabtreebooks.com   1-800-387-7650

Printed in Canada/082016/TL20160715

Published in Canada
Crabtree Publishing
616 Welland Ave.
St. Catharines, Ontario
L2M 5V6

Published in the United States
Crabtree Publishing
PMB 59051
350 Fifth Avenue, 59th Floor
New York, New York 10118

Published in the United Kingdom
Crabtree Publishing
Maritime House
Basin Road North, Hove
BN41 1WR

Published in Australia
Crabtree Publishing
3 Charles Street
Coburg North
VIC, 3058

CONTENTS

CHAPTER ONE

THINK ABOUT IT!

What Is Critical Thinking?

If you were asked to name the main parts of a tree, could you do it? Your answer might include roots, trunk, branches, and leaves or needles. How do you know this is the answer? You might have memorized the parts of a tree in a science class, searched for the answer on Google, or even looked directly at a tree. This question does not require **critical thinking** because the question is simple and so is the answer. If you ask a lot of people this question, many of them would come up with the same answer.

What if you were asked a different question: *How do people depend on plants?* Would this be an easy question to answer? If you ask a lot of people this question, it's unlikely that anyone will have exactly the same answer. This is because the question requires you to **observe** and **analyze** the ways plants are used by people. These are critical-thinking skills. Critical thinking can be approached in many different ways.

It requires you to give evidence and an explanation to explain your thinking.

Critical thinking is a way of solving problems and making decisions by asking questions, gathering information, and using **logic** to make sense of that information. If you make a decision using critical thinking, you can be confident in your decision because you have evidence to back up your reasoning. Practicing critical thinking helps you come up with useful solutions to problems.

What Do You Really Think?

It takes effort to think critically. There are times when you have to **evaluate** claims made by others. Other times, you have to defend your own claims. This requires you to think critically about your own **perspective**. For example: "*I think this music lesson is boring.*" Are you having trouble understanding, and is that why you find it boring? Is it boring because you just don't like the piece you are learning? Or is the lesson boring because you are daydreaming about playing in a band, instead?

CRITICAL THINKING IS A CRUCIAL SKILL IN THE 21ST CENTURY.

21st Century Skills

Our digitally interconnected world is always changing and evolving. To keep up and be successful, we have to be lifelong learners, which means that we must be constantly learning how to think in new and innovative ways. The Partnership for 21st Century Learning is an organization that has identified four essential skills that students need to build to achieve their goals at school, at work, and in their personal lives. They are the 4Cs—communication, collaboration, creativity, and critical thinking. Each skill is important on its own, but combining the four together in our everyday lives is the key to success in a 21st-century world!

Three Types of Thinkers

There are three basic types of thinkers: surface, selfish, and deep.

Surface thinkers prefer not to think too hard or look too far past what is obvious. Usually, they do not think of other perspectives or see anything wrong with their reasoning. They are likely to let others make decisions for them.

Selfish thinkers think a lot—about themselves. They think of ways to persuade others to get what they want, and are less concerned with what is accurate. It's all about "me" for selfish thinkers.

Deep thinkers are critical thinkers. They know their own **limitations.** This means that they are able to see that their personal beliefs might influence a decision they make, and that they can admit when they don't know an answer to a question. Deep thinkers think things through carefully and are willing to consider another person's point of view. They make judgments fairly and **rationally**.

I think this is good enough.

I don't know what to think.

I just can't think of the answer, can you tell me?

What should I tell my friends to get them to back me up on my plan?

How can I get my parents to let me stay up later?

How can I cover up this mistake to avoid getting in trouble?

What is the problem, and how can I best solve it?

Can I trust this source of information?

Do the facts make sense?

> "Think left and think right
> And think low and think high.
> Oh, the thinks you can think
> If only you try!"
>
> *Children's author*
> *Dr Seuss*

Decision Time

In reality, our decision-making is sometimes surface, sometimes selfish, and sometimes deep. There are times when we make quick decisions without thinking, such as accepting an invitation to go to a friend's house for dinner. There are times when we are selfish, such as deciding not to accept a dinner invitation because you like what you're having for dinner at your house better. Deep thinking is usually saved for big decisions, such as deciding whether you should look for a job to start making money or spend time fine-tuning your piano-playing talent.

Why Is Critical Thinking Important?

Critical thinking is a valuable skill to build early in life. In school, memorizing the solution to a problem means you can answer that same problem every time. But if you learn how to tackle problems using critical thinking instead, you gain tools that allow you to solve a wide variety of problems.

Get Writing Right

Critical thinking can develop your writing skills. It helps you:

Be clear about your **argument** or point of view

Support your conclusions

Follow a clear line of reasoning

Use evidence to support your reasoning

Read your own work critically

Recognize what works well and what doesn't

Come up with ways to improve your work

Daily Decisions

The usefulness of critical thinking goes beyond school into daily life. If your friend asks you to come over and play a video game that your parents have said you can't play because it is too violent, then your answer is clear. But if you have never been told to not play that game, you might need to think critically about whether it is appropriate. Do your friend's parents approve of them playing it? Is the rating appropriate for your age? Do you think your parents would mind you playing this game? Is this something you will enjoy or will you just be saying yes to make your friend happy? Once you've gathered some information and figured it out in your mind, then you can make a justified decision based on facts.

Information Explosion

Today, technology is changing rapidly. With the increase of information available at our fingertips, it is becoming more important than ever to have a method for organizing and evaluating information. We need to weigh the **relevance** and **reliability** of the information we find when searching for answers to questions or problems. This helps us make thoughtful and accurate decisions.

CHAPTER TWO

THE ART OF ASKING QUESTIONS

What Do We Mean by Critical?

What came to mind when you first heard the term **critical thinking**? Did you focus on the word critical? Did you think that if you are thinking critically, you are looking for flaws in something you have read, heard, or watched?

Critical thinking does not mean negative thinking. Critical in this case relates to the word criteria, which refers to standards by which something may be judged or decided on. Critical thinkers are looking for answers to questions in order to find the best solutions for problems.

What's the Big Picture?

Critical thinking means being able to question and evaluate information to determine whether it is accurate, reliable, or useful. It is a way of thinking that goes beyond the obvious facts. Critical thinking encourages you to look at the big picture, which includes everything surrounding the topic.

To help you look at the whole picture, whatever the issue is, start by asking questions that begin with:

- ? **What...?**
- ? **How...?**
- ? **When...?**
- ? **Who...?**
- ? **Why...? and**
- ? **What if...?**

Asking the right kinds of questions will help you form your own **opinion** and come to a conclusion based on reasoning.

CRITICAL THINKING COVERS ALL THINKING PROCESSES BELOW THE SURFACE

Critical thinking is a term that covers all thinking processes that strive to dig below the surface of something: questioning, **probing**, analyzing, testing, and exploring. Critical thinking requires detective-like skills of persistence to examine and reexamine an argument in order to take in all the angles and consider evidence from every side.

SPOTLIGHT

There is little doubt that the Greek **philosopher** Socrates was a deep thinker. Socrates developed and taught a method of thinking that uses questioning to determine how reasonable an idea is.

Socrates found that many people could not back up their claims when they were carefully questioned. He promoted the importance of seeking evidence, closely examining reasoning and **assumptions**, studying all aspects of a question, and figuring out the **implications** of things that are said and done. Today, this is what we call critical thinking.

"To find yourself, think for yourself."
Socrates

Top Traits of a Critical Thinker

What do an **investigative journalist**, a crime-scene detective, and a philosopher have in common? They all share the characteristics of critical thinkers.

Critical thinkers:

- (?) are curious and eager to learn more

- (?) are problem solvers

- (?) are capable of asking appropriate questions

- (?) seek evidence to support assumptions and beliefs

- (?) are able to distinguish between fact and opinion

- (?) can admit when they do not understand or if there is not enough information to come to a conclusion

- (?) are careful and active observers

- (?) look for proof

- (?) are open to new ideas and changing their positions

- (?) are thoughtful

- (?) listen carefully to others and are able to give feedback

- (?) see critical thinking as a lifelong process of self-discovery and awareness.

Getting to the Truth

Good critical thinkers are willing to listen to others. They enjoy hearing different points of view and **debating** issues. They value arguments built with solid reasoning that form sound conclusions. Good critical thinkers are confident in their abilities to reason. Above all, they are curious. They want to uncover the truth—even when the truth might challenge their own beliefs, and when the truth might not be in their own best interest.

Critical thinkers try to develop qualities called **intellectual virtues**. These include:

- (?) perseverance—sticking to a problem despite setbacks

- (?) independence—trying to think for yourself

- (?) integrity—trying to be the kind of person you expect others to be

- (?) empathy—trying to understand how other people feel

- (?) humility—admitting you don't know everything

- (?) courage—speaking up for what is right, even if it is not easy.

HANDS ON

Are you a rock or a feather? This challenge gets you to make choices and examine your own reasoning, and the ways your friends make and support their decisions.

Materials needed:

A group of friends

Challenge:

1. Give your friends the following pairs of words. Ask them to explain how each pair is related, and how they are different. For example: black/orange—both are colors, but one is dark and one is bright.

river/lake
sunshine/rain
spring/fall
guitar/banjo
apple/orange
house/apartment
bedroom/kitchen
up/down
right/wrong

2. Now repeat the exercise with rock/feather. Think about the similarities and differences between these two words. Then ask your friends if they think they are a rock or a feather. Listen to each other as you explain your decisions. There are no right or wrong answers! But by answering this question, you and your friends are forced to make a choice and examine the qualities that support that decision.

13

Becoming a Critical Thinker

Every day we have to solve problems and answer questions that require strong critical-thinking skills. When you write an essay at school, you need to plan your writing by organizing your ideas. To do this, you should rank each idea in order of importance.

If you were applying for a part-time job stocking shelves in a local corner store, you probably need to write a résumé. It would be good to list your skills in order of how closely they relate to this job. Volunteering in the local library reshelving books would be more relevant than babysitting.

However, not all critical thinking is straightforward. Take the popular TV show *Survivor*. Players use critical thinking to decide which player to vote off next. Groups form and members must trust one another to vote the same way. Emotion and **ego** often get in the way of clear critical thinking.

Critical thinking means processing your thoughts in a clear and logical way.

Break Down the Barriers

There are many barriers to critical thinking. Knowing what these are—and being able to recognize them in ourselves—is the first step to breaking them down. So, what are some of the barriers?

Going with instinct rather than thinking about decisions.

Thinking we know it all and therefore not asking questions.

Being unwilling to listen.

Not reviewing mistakes.

Wanting to be given answers rather than figuring them out.

Believing that some people or ideas are better than others.

Facing social pressure.

Assuming that things are true without proof.

Make It Your Own

Take 10-15 minutes every day and practice critical thinking. Think about any decisions you made during the day. If you could remake any of those decisions, would you change anything? If so, what—and why?

Some people are naturally better at critical thinking than others. But critical thinking is a skill that anyone can practice, improve, and strengthen over time. You just have to be willing to make the effort.

Learning to Ask Good Questions

Every choice you make is based on what you know at the time you make that choice. If you are offered a lime-flavored drink or an orange-flavored drink, you might choose orange because you like that taste better. But if you knew that the orange-flavored drink was artificially flavored and colored whereas the lime-flavored drink was completely natural, you might choose differently. And what if you knew that most people preferred the lime-flavored drink over the orange-flavored one? Would that influence your decision? You would not have known these things if you didn't ask questions, such as *"Are they artificially or naturally flavored?"* or *"Which one do you think tastes better?"* and *"Why?"* Critical thinking can clear away confusion by simply questioning statements and assumptions.

Finding the Right Question

Critical thinking is all about understanding that there are always questions that need to be answered. The questions themselves need to be clear and precise. Here's a list of good questions to help you start thinking critically:

- What would happen if…?
- How is this similar to…?
- What was the point of…?
- What else could be done differently?
- How would you feel if…?
- How could you improve…?
- Could there be different points of view? What would they be?
- Could some people interpret this differently? How?

WHAT DO I NEED TO KNOW?

? Are you interested in finding out the truth?

? Are you open to new ideas, even though you might not initially agree with them?

? Do you act **impulsively**, or try to look at the pros and cons before making a decision?

? Do you break difficult problems into manageable pieces?

? Are you confident in your reasons for decisions or are you likely to back down when questioned by others?

? Are you curious?

? Do you try to see things from other people's viewpoints?

Getting Started

Thinking critically about solving a problem starts with asking questions. To ask useful questions, try these tips:

- ❓ Be clear at the start of the process about what you are trying to achieve

- ❓ Try to understand exactly what the problem is, from all angles

- ❓ Ask for explanations and examples when you don't understand something

- ❓ Don't get discouraged—it's okay to be confused and ask questions!

For example, imagine you are trying to help a friend who is upset. You want to help, but first you need to understand the problem they are dealing with. In this situation, it's helpful to use questions to help you understand. Did they fail a test? Are their feelings hurt by something someone said or did? Were they cut from a team tryout? Once you figure out the problem, try to understand their point of view. What support or help can you offer?

A good friend who is really upset may not make any sense when you try to talk to them, or may even push you away. If you want to help and support them, try to find a way to understand their feelings. Being compassionate, or understanding others' feelings, is part of critical thinking.

Stay on Track

It is okay to discuss other topics that relate to the problem, but remain focused and stay on track. Ask yourself if there are better or different ways to answer the question. Make sure any extra information is related and meaningful to the question you are trying to answer, or the problem you are trying to solve.

Searching for patterns and ways that things fit together is a logical approach to problem solving. Be prepared to answer questions about how you came to a specific conclusion. But also remember there may not be an answer to the question—the problem may not be able to be solved.

HANDS ON

How quickly can you make connections? This challenge tests valuable critical-thinking skills: your ability to look for patterns, and see how things are connected.

Materials needed:
A timer or stopwatch and a few friends

Challenge:
First try this on your own, then test your friends. How fast can you find the connection between these sets of words?

flake/man/ball
clothing/jewelry/department
video/board/card

*Hint: What one word can you add to each set to make a new word or phrase?

Critical thinking, like a good game of chess, requires evaluating each step.

CHAPTER THREE

FINDING ANSWERS

Gathering Information

All **research** has a purpose. When we think critically, research can provide the information we need to solve a problem or answer a question. Research includes data, information, or evidence. When we conduct research, we make **inferences** from which we later draw conclusions.

What does it mean to draw conclusions from inferences? Suppose someone says: "*The only place I have ever seen a cactus growing is in the desert. I think that is the only place they grow.*"

This person has based their conclusion, that cacti only grow in deserts, on an inference— that they have only seen cacti grow in deserts. Is that true?

You do a little research and find out that most cacti grow in desert environments. Your mom reminds you that there is a huge cactus growing in the yard of your grandparents' home. You even discover a tiny cactus growing in an indoor garden at your friend's home. These facts prove that although cacti grow in the desert, they can be found elsewhere, too.

Looking for Answers

When you have a problem or question, the next logical step is to look for answers. Say that your family is planning to visit another country for the summer. You want to know if it will be a positive experience. Where would you go to find out more information? What facts would you need to know? Searching for information or facts can lead you to a logical answer to your question.

Everybody has his or her own point of view when starting research. We all have some level of background knowledge, as well as our own ideas and opinions. Most of us have a foundation of knowledge from media sources such as television and radio news programs, newspapers, and blogs. Even if you do not listen to the news often, you can get your knowledge by talking with your friends, connecting on Facebook or Twitter, or even watching reality TV shows. Our ideas and opinions can also be influenced by what we see in advertisements and read in magazines.

YOU CAN FIND INFORMATION BY TALKING TO PEOPLE WITH PERSONAL EXPERIENCES OR USING YOUR OWN PERSONAL EXPERIENCES.

SPOTLIGHT

Carl Sagan was an astronomer and author interested in the scientific research of extraterrestrial life. He wrote over 600 scientific papers and articles and close to two dozen books. He asked questions about life outside of our planet and did research to search for proof that alien life-forms exist. Carl Sagan was a critical thinker.

"I don't want to believe, I want to know."
Carl Sagan

Check Your Facts

The next step is to carefully research your facts. Always check to see if the information you are receiving is true. Are there any mistakes in your reasoning? Do not assume that everything is true when searching for the information you need to solve the problem. Remember:

FACTS are true statements that can be proven.

OPINIONS are statements that cannot be proven.

An opinion is what someone thinks is right, but opinions are often based on feelings and emotions. It is important to remember that two people can have completely different opinions on the same topic:

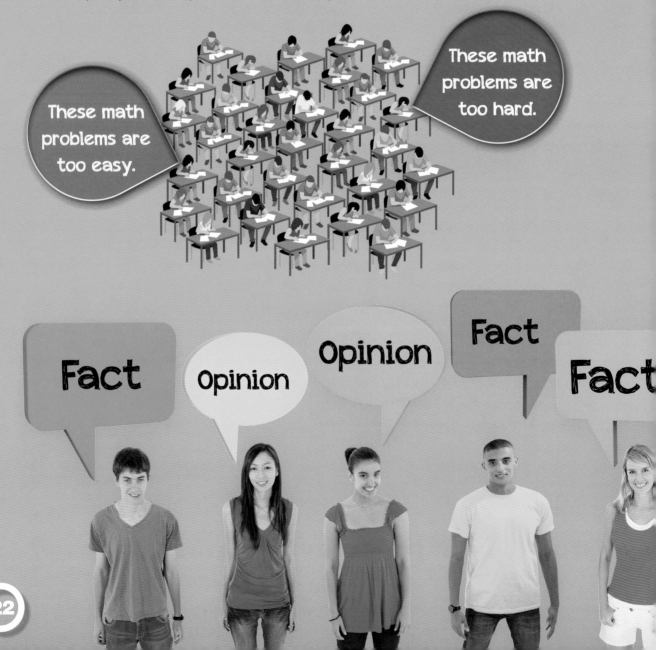

Question Yourself

It is easy to listen to a comment or presentation and assume that all of the information given is true. It's important to consider whether the speaker has evidence to back up their words. When we notice and question our assumptions, it helps reveal gaps in logic or the fact that there is not enough information.

When you are gathering information, use logic to think about your assumptions beforehand. Do you assume that your best friend always has reliable information? Is there evidence to back that up? Learn to see gaps in your logic, and look out for opinions presented as facts. Test yourself and see if you can write one fact and one opinion about yourself, such as *"I live in... [name of place you live]."* and *"I am the funniest person in my class."*

Fact or Opinion?

It takes skill to learn how to tell the difference between facts and opinions. Read each sentence below and decide whether it is a fact or an opinion. Write your answers down on a sheet of paper.

1. Oceans are more beautiful than mountains.

2. The blue whale is the largest mammal on Earth.

3. Leftover pizza is yummy.

4. My sister is silly.

5. I lost my house key.

6. Apples and oranges are types of fruit.

7. Blue is the prettiest color.

8. I am expecting my parents to arrive by five o'clock.

9. Birds lay eggs.

10. Chickens are nice, but roosters are not.

(Answers: 1-O, 2-F, 3-O, 4-O, 5-F, 6-F, 7-O, 8-F, 9-F, 10-O)

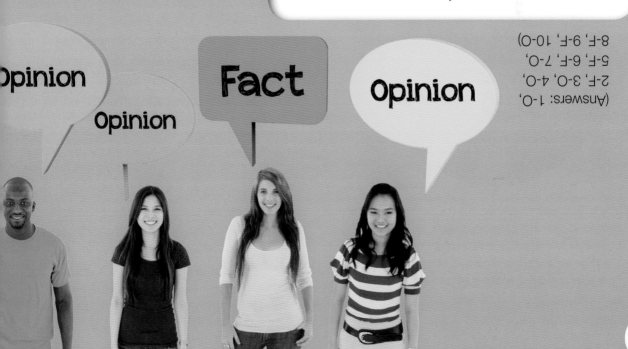

Opinion

Opinion

Fact

Opinion

There are many different places to find answers. Many people start their research online.

Online Research

Where would you start your research? The Internet? There's nothing wrong with that, as long as you think before you click.

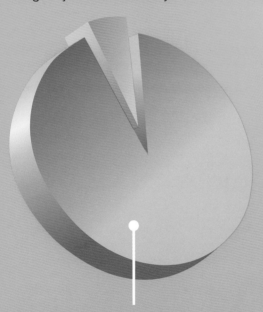

Around 95 percent of young people aged 12 to 17 are online. It's important to remember that not all websites are equal when it comes to providing reliable information.

First, ask yourself if you believe everything you see on TV. Of course not! What about the Internet? Do you think that everything you see, read, or listen to online is the truth? The Internet offers a mix of opinions and facts, but it may not always be easy to tell the difference. Anyone can put information on the Internet and present it as fact. For example, you do not have to have be a doctor to start a website giving medical advice—a scary thought! It is important to know the source of Internet information and get in the habit of asking where the information comes from.

The pie chart on the left shows the high percentage of 12- to 17-year-olds who are online and the small percentage (around 5 percent) who are not. Numbers like these are called statistics. Statistics are facts or data taken from a survey or study of people or things. Always check the survey or study was carried out by a **credible** source—sometimes people manipulate statistics to make a point.

Credibility Check

When finding answers online, always ask yourself:

Does this website help with my understanding of the question or problem?

Where does the information come from? (Checking the "about us" or "who we are" links may help you find out which person or group created the site.)

What is the point of view?

What information is missing?

Are certain people and opinions not represented?

"Expert" Advice?

Would you believe a website if the author uses a false title or name, such as Dr Know-It-All or Miss Etiquette? It is important to know who people are before using their information. Sometimes people leave comments on websites using the name "anonymous." If they are not willing to identify themselves, why should we believe their opinions? They must also be an authority on the topic. Would you immediately trust a response about climate change from a bus driver? The information given by the "expert" must fit in with a majority of experts. In other words, if one expert is saying that **Bigfoot** exists, but every other expert says that there is no such thing as Bigfoot, would you still believe the first expert?

WARNING

BIGFOOT IN THIS AREA

Is It Valuable?

We are constantly coming up against the perspectives, opinions, and ideas of other people. What is true? What is useful? This is where critical thinking, using reasoning and evidence, helps you come to a decision.

Questions to Ask

Who said that?

Is that source reliable?

Do they have facts supporting that claim?

Has that been scientifically proven?

Are they qualified to speak on this topic?

Are they telling the complete truth, or are they telling you what is best for their own interests?

Do you need to ask further questions?

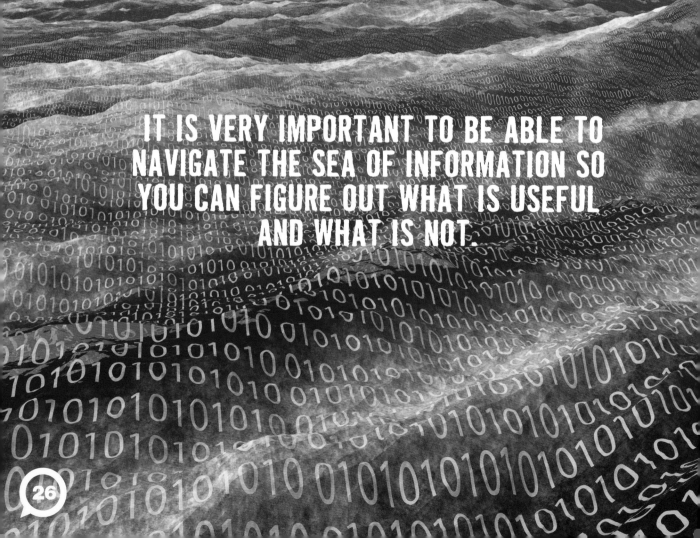

IT IS VERY IMPORTANT TO BE ABLE TO NAVIGATE THE SEA OF INFORMATION SO YOU CAN FIGURE OUT WHAT IS USEFUL AND WHAT IS NOT.

Weak Links

Some evidence is strong, but a lot can be weak when examined. Be careful to:

- **(?)** check the date of any research (Is it recent, or old, and therefore no longer relevant?)

- **(?)** check the sources of information

- **(?)** check that statistics are convincing—numbers, such as percentages, can be used to make weak data look better

- **(?)** beware of words that try to sound like statistics (for example, "most people")

- **(?)** look out for words that try to convince you that something is true (such as "obviously" or "surely").

If you think critically and focus, the Internet is great. If you don't, it can be a source of misinformation and distraction.

Busting Internet Myths

Have you ever seen the TV show *Mythbusters*? It's centered around investigating and testing popular myths to see if they are based in fact. When you surf the Internet, you sometimes have to be a "myth buster" yourself, to judge whether what you are reading is fact or fiction. Ask questions. Check out the reliability of the source. Do alligators live in sewers under New York City? No. This is an urban myth. Just because you read something on the Internet doesn't mean that it is true.

Compare and contrast one site against another. Does the information match? Are the statements and ideas backed by facts? Are reliable experts quoted? If you can't find answers to these questions, you have reason to doubt the information. Dig deeper. You may find that what you are reading is not really true.

Don't believe everything you hear—or read!

Mapping It Out

Gathering information can be overwhelming. Think about writing an essay about a topic. You need to gather information from many different sources. It takes time to look through all of the pieces of information you have collected and examine connections between them. In order to decide the best way to organize your ideas, you need to be able to see the advantages, disadvantages, and possible consequences of placing more emphasis on some facts than others.

A mind map or concept map is a good way to collect all those things in one place. It helps provide a clear picture.

A mind map is a type of diagram where ideas and information branch off from a central question or problem. Creating a mind map requires critical-thinking skills to organize thoughts and information. Some mind mappers use different colors for every main branch of their map. This gives them a better overview of the whole problem or question.

Mind maps:

- ❓ don't tie you to one point of view
- ❓ are great for **brainstorming**
- ❓ organize your ideas
- ❓ help work out key relationships
- ❓ help connect new ideas to previous knowledge
- ❓ show connections.

HANDS ON

This challenge will get you to practice your mapping skills.

Materials needed:

Paper and pens

Challenge:

Create a mind map to help answer the following question:

You are going to be stranded on an island with another person. You have the choice of taking someone physically fit, someone smart, or someone caring and supportive with you. Who will you take?

Start by putting this main question in a circle in the middle of your paper. Draw lines out to three separate circles, then write each choice inside. Now add circles to each that list the pros and cons of being physically fit, smart, or caring and supportive. Look at your map. Does laying out the information help you make a decision? Do you need to ask more questions?

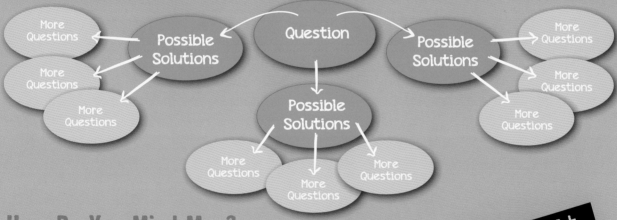

How Do You Mind Map?

Start with a blank piece of paper. In the center, write down the key question (or problem). You might want to circle this to make it stand out. You could also add an image to make it memorable.

Add additional keywords (or subtopics) around your key question. Write simple phrases to support a keyword.

You may choose to use different colors or shapes to represent different elements. You could use one color to represent facts or evidence, another to show your opinion, and another to represent your arguments.

Make It Your Own

Map out your understanding of critical thinking so far!

CHAPTER FOUR

MINDFUL THINKING

What Is Mindful Thinking?

Mindfulness means being aware of something in the present moment. It means that you are in tune with your thoughts and feelings, and that you pay attention to them without making judgments about them. You might think you are practicing mindful thinking all of the time, but that's rarely the case! Our minds tend to wander all over the place, and our decisions are often **unconsciously** affected by our ego, assumptions, or **bias**. Mindful thinking means being aware of these kinds of limitations, and thinking about a problem from all sorts of perspectives.

Lose the Ego

Critical thinking is an attempt to answer questions by reasoning them out. This means thinking, understanding, and forming judgments in a logical manner. However, we don't always do this! Sometimes we answer whatever comes first to mind. This is often related to our ego.

Ego is the "I" in our thoughts, such as *"I am hungry."* Each one of us is at the center of our own life experiences and we tend to put ourselves first. Our lives are influenced by how we think, and how we think is affected by our life experiences. It is easy to tell yourself that your decisions are going to be good for someone else, but in reality your decisions are often made in your own best interest. When this happens, it is hard to be fair to others in our decision-making.

There are times when our ego makes us fearful: *"I will look foolish if I do that."* The fear of making mistakes can make it difficult to try something new. Critical thinking invites you to overcome the ego's fear and develop what some people call **intellectual courage**.

It takes courage to risk making a mistake, but making mistakes is part of the process of critical thinking. Like any new skill, it takes practice to think critically and do it well. The key is to learn from your mistakes. In doing so, you might find new and creative ways to solve old problems.

IT CAN TAKE COURAGE TO LOSE OUR EGO AND TRY SOMETHING NEW OR TAKE A DIFFERENT PATH.

SPOTLIGHT

As a child, Nelson Mandela had dreamed of helping black people find equality in South Africa, where **apartheid** meant that they were treated as lower-class citizens. As an adult, Mandela spent nearly 30 years in prison for challenging apartheid and fighting for equal rights for all people. He did not just question the old way of thinking; he was a critical thinker. He considered the problems in South Africa from many points of view in order to bring people together and find solutions. In 1994, Nelson Mandela became the first black president of South Africa.

"I like friends who have independent minds because they tend to make you see problems from all angles."

Nelson Mandela

Listen Up!

You may not notice, but while you are speaking your mind is busy arranging words and the order in which they come out of your mouth. What we are saying makes total sense to us. However, it can sometimes be difficult to make sense of what someone else is saying. We are not inside that person's head. We do not have their point of view.

Imagine watching a movie with a group of friends. You reach for another handful of popcorn and one friend blurts out: *"World hunger."* Huh? Your other friends shrug their shoulders and continue watching the movie. Some people listen passively and uncritically. They do not question or try to understand.

Critical thinkers use **active listening**. They ask questions if they are not sure what the other person means, such as *"I'm not sure I understand"* or *"What do you mean?"* In this case, you might just ask your friend: *"What about world hunger?"* Your friend goes on to say that they were looking at the bowl of popcorn and thinking about how lucky we are to have food to snack on whenever we want.

You tell them you still don't get it. You friend goes on to say, *"Remember in class today when the teacher was talking about picking topics for the group project tomorrow? We should do a project on world hunger."* Now you can understand what your friend was thinking, and you can evaluate their idea to decide whether you agree. Thinking involves active listening.

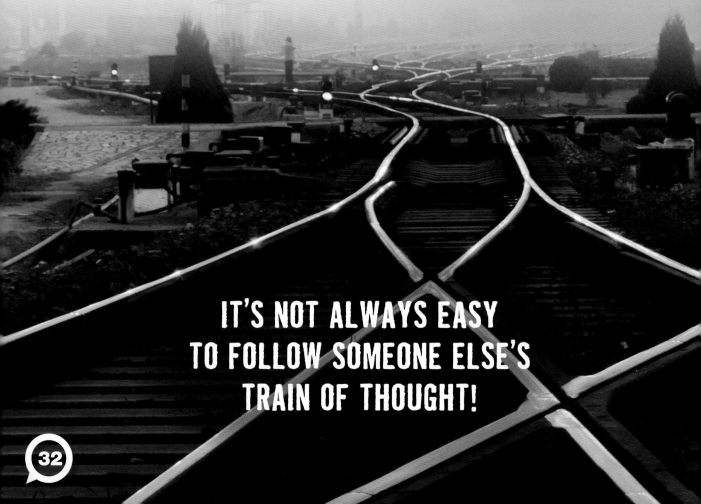

IT'S NOT ALWAYS EASY
TO FOLLOW SOMEONE ELSE'S
TRAIN OF THOUGHT!

What Is Active Listening?

Active listening means giving the speaker your whole attention without being distracted. Then, you can understand what they are saying and respond. Understanding what someone is saying can be very different to just hearing what they have said.

Remove distractions

Stay focused on the speaker and maintain eye contact

Try to understand how the speaker is feeling

Ask questions to help you understand, but don't interrupt or make assumptions

Active listening

Give feedback to the speaker to ensure you understand

I think that...

So what you are saying is...

Yes or No—or Maybe?

All or nothing.

Us versus them.

The issues are black and white.

How many times have you heard people say things like this? These are very general, simple statements that can apply to a lot of situations. The problem with these kinds of **generalizations** is that they oversimplify complex issues that have more than just two sides. Rather than trying to understand the big picture, these sayings provide excuses for not thinking things all the way through.

People who do not think critically often see the answers to questions as yes or no. By doing so, they fail to see that there may be many layers to an issue. They believe the facts they already know are the only relevant ones and do not try to understand any other perspectives.

In reality, not all answers are black and white—there is a whole lot of gray! Critical thinking means a commitment to seeing both sides of an issue. It means embracing the "maybe"—and trying to find a truth that may be somewhere in the middle.

HANDS ON

This challenge provides you with the opportunity to think about different possibilities.

Premise:
You have $1000 to donate toward hunger relief. Which organization will you support?

Challenge:
You can use any resources you wish, but you must **justify** your reasoning. Think about these questions as you go through the decision-making process:

- What information do I need to answer my question?
- What is my point of view on the issue of world hunger?
- Do I have any biases?
- What assumptions am I using in my reasoning? Are my assumptions correct?

Test Yourself

Imagine that you and a friend have arranged to work on a school project each weekend. Then your friend skips two weeks in a row. You wonder how to deal with the situation.

What do you do?

Ignore your friend and complain about their behavior to your teacher, other friends, and anyone who will listen.

Ask them why.

They mumble that they had something else to do.

What do you do now?

Get mad at them or storm off. They clearly don't care about you or the project!

Ask them more questions to try and understand their perspective.

You might discover that there is a good reason for their actions. Perhaps a family member is sick, and they weren't comfortable talking about it. You and your friend figure out a new schedule that will work for the both of you.

We do not always see things clearly at first. Our own self-interests need to be set aside, which can be hard to do when you are learning to think critically. You must learn to see things as they really are, not how you think they should be. You have to remember that the goal is to find the best answer—not just the answer that is best for you.

CHAPTER FIVE

EVALUATING ARGUMENTS

What Is an Argument?

An "argument" doesn't just mean a heated discussion between two people. An argument can also be an attempt to convince someone that something is true.

Being able to spot, make, and evaluate these types of arguments is central to critical thinking. So, how do you start?

Stop arguing!

This isn't an argument!

It isn't!

It is!

Look, this study proves that teenagers have different sleep patterns. They'd benefit from a later start.

No way.

School should start later for teenagers.

Really? Let me see that!

Here are some more facts...

Claims and Conclusions

An argument is made up of two parts: a claim (or claims) and a conclusion. The person making the argument gives a set of claims as reasons to convince others that they should accept the conclusion. In the conversation on page 36, the claim is that teenagers have different sleep patterns, so a later school start time would be better for them. The argument ends with the speaker about to make more claims. The conclusion is that school should start later for teenagers.

If someone is trying to convince you to believe something, it is important to remember that it is their responsibility to make their claims and conclusion clear and complete. If you cannot understand the claims or conclusion of someone's argument, then you cannot evaluate their argument. You cannot accept the conclusion of an argument you don't understand.

True, False, or Unknown?

Read each argument below. Accept that the claims of the argument are true. What is the conclusion? Do you agree? Start by deciding if each statement is true, false, or unknown.

Kyle and his teammates are playing a hockey game at the local arena against the second-best team in the division.

Kyle's team has lost only two games in the last year.

Kyle's team will win the game.

1. Kyle plays hockey. Is this statement true, false, or unknown?

2. There is a hockey game being played at the local arena. True, false, or unknown?

3. Kyle's team will win the game. True, false, or unknown?

Evaluation Checklist

When evaluating an argument, first check you fully understand the argument. Then use criteria, such as the **FELT** checklist below, to help you with your evaluation.

FAIRNESS Does the argument seem balanced and fair, or is it one-sided? Look out for hints of bias, such as a narrow viewpoint or language, that show emotions such as anger.

EVIDENCE Are the claims fully explained? Are they supported with evidence? Are there any contradictions in the argument, or any evidence that proves the conclusion is wrong? Does the author include other points of view, and explain why they support or do not support the main argument?

LOGIC Do the claims lead logically to the conclusion?

TONE Does the author's tone of voice, or the way they speak, seem appropriate for the argument? For example, is it calm and clear, or unnecessarily emotional, sarcastic, or dramatic?

Avoid Assumptions

Think back to that case of your friend not meeting you to work on the school project. If you had assumed they were purposely avoiding work, instead of asking questions to understand their perspective, you might have damaged the friendship or got them into trouble at school. Then imagine how you would feel when you found out the true facts of the case. You would probably regret making that assumption. It is important to think things through before acting based on assumptions.

Make It Your Own

Look at this photograph. What conclusions might you make about the person in it?

Did you assume the person in the photo was a refugee or someone without a home? Why? How does your interpretation of the photo change when you find out that this person is someone fighting for a cause?

What's the Evidence?

In the activity above, you made an inference about the person in the photo. When you infer something, it means you draw a conclusion based on evidence. Take the following example:

You leave a chocolate bar on the kitchen counter and leave the house. Your older sister is the only one in the house. When you come back, the chocolate bar is gone. What do you think happened? You might infer that she ate the chocolate bar. Extra evidence comes from the fact that there is a crumpled-up wrapper in the trash can in her bedroom!

What's the Real Story?

Based on the evidence you had, you inferred that your sister had eaten the chocolate bar. What you did not know was that your dad came home early from work. He grabbed the chocolate bar off the kitchen counter, started devouring it while he spoke with your sister in her bedroom, and threw the empty wrapper in her trash can.

In this case, you made a judgment before you had all the facts. If you had asked your sister directly, she would have told you the whole story.

How Good a Judge Are You?

Some people are better than others when it comes to pulling together information to arrive at a logical conclusion. They are often characterized as having "good judgment" because they typically arrive at a good decision. They are also able to change their position when the evidence supports doing so.

Read the following short scene and then make inferences, or conclusions, based on the evidence:

Your friend walks past you with a big frown. She is shaking her head from side to side. She looks at her report card again, then jams it into her backpack. What do you infer? What evidence supports your conclusion?

Practice Makes Perfect

With practice, we begin to see that the inferences we make are influenced by our point of view and the assumptions we make about people and situations. We learn to see situations, problems, or questions from more than one point of view. This allows us to become more fair and open-minded.

We make assumptions all the time. Many of our inferences are justified and reasonable. Some are not. Being aware that our inferences may not always be justified is one of the most important critical-thinking skills.

Explaining Your Choice

When you use critical thinking, you are able to use evidence and reasoning to explain your conclusions and decisions. This is the payoff for all of your hard work. When you think critically, the big picture becomes clear. This helps you make tough decisions, or solve difficult problems with justifiable reasons. You should be able to explain how you came to your decision clearly, and in your own words.

Arguing your point—and being able to evaluate the arguments of others—are important steps in critical thinking.

Know Your Audience

It's important that your decision is fully understood by anyone you are sharing it with. This means that you need to know your audience and explain your decisions and conclusions in a way that makes sense to them.

Imagine you are giving two speeches about fundraising ideas for your school trip to Europe. One of those speeches is for close friends and family. They already know why you are trying to raise money. All you need to do is convince them to sponsor you.

The other speech is for the local symphony. They sometimes sponsor students looking to expand their knowledge of music through travel. This group needs more information to understand the "who, what, where, when, how, and why" behind your trip. To convince them, you need to give evidence to support your reasons about how the trip will expand your music knowledge.

Your ability to clearly explain your ideas, while keeping in mind your audience, is important for making sure your information is understood and well received.

CHAPTER SIX

TAKING CHARGE

I Own That!

No one can think critically for you. That means you have to be aware of your own thinking abilities and tear things apart to find deeper answers and meaning. In other words, critical thinking is all up to you!

If you work on it, your critical-thinking skills will continue to improve. It won't happen overnight and it won't always be easy. There might be times you feel as though your judgment is getting worse instead of better, and you may doubt your ability. Tough problems and hard situations can be discouraging.

At first, you might get slowed down by the decision-making process. That's because you have to change the way you approach a problem in the first place. You have to get rid of certain habits and learn new ones. It's like learning a new sport, instrument, or language—learning to think critically takes time and practice.

This challenge will help you practice finding evidence and creating a strong argument.

Materials needed:

Four to six friends so you can work in two small groups to debate an issue.

Challenge:

You are going to debate the following question: *Should we stop making products out of plastic?*

Split into two groups and each take a side (yes or no). Make sure you understand the statement, then research and find specific information to support your side of the debate.

Once you have done your research and feel prepared, have a debate*. Make sure you explain your position clearly and support it with strong evidence.

After the debate, evaluate how it went. What worked well in your argument? Was your evidence valuable and reliable? What would you do differently next time you debate an issue?

*Remember that debates only work when participants use respect and fairness. Make sure everyone has a chance to speak, and do not interrupt another participant.

YOU HAVE THE KNOWLEDGE NOW. YOU KNOW WHAT CRITICAL THINKING IS ALL ABOUT. WHERE WILL YOU TAKE IT FROM HERE?

Make It Your Own

See if you can explain your position to your friends, and then to a parent or other family member. Your explanation should be different in each case, since they will probably have two different levels of knowledge on the topic. In the end, both groups should have a similar understanding of the subject.

A Lifelong Journey

We need to build on and improve our critical-thinking skills throughout our lives. These skills are important not only in our school life, but in our personal lives and eventually our work lives as well. Critical thinkers think and act using strong reason and evidence to support their thoughts.

Critical-thinking skills go hand in hand with creativity, communication, and collaboration. To come up with new and creative solutions to problems, it is necessary to work with others and learn to communicate well. All of these skills are key to a successful future.

TED (Technology, Entertainment, and Design) is a worldwide community of people who are looking for a deeper understanding of the world. A nonprofit organization, TED believes in the power of ideas and is devoted to spreading those ideas, usually in the form of short talks.

Tavi Gevinson is a 15-year-old who is still figuring out what makes a strong female role model. She questioned what we consider role models and looked for answers. Tavi realized that one question led to another and to another...and so the title of her TED talk is "Still figuring it out." Tavi is the perfect example of a critical thinker using the TED Talk platform to share her ideas and continue her search for answers.

Tavi created a blog at the age of 11 to express her interpretation of the fashion world. A role model for many youth, she encourages everyone to search for their own answers on what makes

TED Talks releases the best TED content online, for free. Talks are meant to stir your curiosity and spark conversation, but all science and health information must be supported by valid research. This is not a place for one-sided arguments. What is the magical ingredient that brings Pixar movies to life? How could humans evolve to survive in space? What are the surprising habits of original thinkers? How did African youth find a voice on Twitter? Could you see yourself becoming a TED speaker in the future? What topics will you address?

You have mastered the basics of critical thinking, but it is far from over. Learning is a lifelong journey. Critical thinking is a process that grows with you and continues to enrich your understanding throughout life. It begins with a question or problem that is understood, investigated and evaluated, and answered or solved with reason. Where will your questions take you next?

"Critical thinking is thinking about your thinking while you're thinking in order to make your thinking better."
Richard W. Paul, critical-thinking scholar

GLOSSARY

active listening A way of listening and responding that helps you clearly understand a message

analyze To examine something carefully in order to understand it

apartheid A government policy based on racial separation and discrimination

argument A set of reasons that support an idea or opinion

assumptions General beliefs that something is true, without knowing for sure

bias Prejudice for or against something or someone; a preconceived judgment not based in fact

Bigfoot A mythological, large, hairy beast found in North America

brainstorming Quickly coming up with and recording ideas without judging them, often in a group

credible Reliable; able to be taken as fact

critical thinking Thinking clearly and logically about something in order to form a judgment

debating Discussing something formally

ego The "I" or self of a person

evaluate Form an idea of the value of something

generalizations General statements or ideas gathered by inference

implications The meaning, consequences, or significance of something

impulsively Describing an action that is sudden and not thought through

inferences Conclusions made after considering the facts or evidence given

intellectual courage Standing by ideas, beliefs, or views no matter what

intellectual virtues The qualities, such as critical thinking, that someone cultivates through learning and training their mind

investigative journalist A reporter who researches, or investigates, a story covering all the angles

justify To try and prove that your words or actions are right

limitations The points beyond which someone cannot go

logic Good reasoning or thinking

observe To notice something of significance

opinion Your personal feelings about something or someone

perspective A way of looking at something

philosopher A person who searches for truth, wisdom, and knowledge

probing Looking carefully to uncover information

rationally Describing something that is based on facts or reason

relevance The amount to which something is useful or connected to a topic

reliability Being able to be trusted or depended upon

research Investigation into something in order to get facts and reach conclusions

unconsciously Describing an action that is done without realizing or without conscious thought

LEARNING MORE

Books

Analogies for Critical Thinking Grade 5 by Ruth Foster.
Teacher Created Resources, 2011.

Critical Thinking Skills For Dummies by Martin Cohen.
John Wiley & Sons, Ltd., 2015.

Reading Detective A1 by Cheryl Block.
The Critical Thinking Co., 2013.

Think: Why You Should Question Everything by Guy P. Harrison.
Prometheus Books, 2013.

Websites

Brain Boosters
http://school.discoveryeducation.com/brainboosters
Visit this page from Discovery Education to find lots of logic and reasoning activities.

101 Activities for Teaching Creativity and Problem Solving
www.bio-nica.info/biblioteca/VanGoundy2005101ActivitiesTeaching.pdf
This guide to 101 activities is from Bio-Nica, a resource from Nicaragua that includes an online library.

50 Activities for Developing Critical Thinking Skills
http://spers.ca/wp-content/uploads/2013/08/50-activities-for-developing-critical-thinking-skills.pdf
Try some of these activities to improve and cultivate your critical-thinking skills!

TED Talks
www.ted.com/playlists/129/ted_under_20
Listen to talks by young, bright minds in the fields of science, innovation, music, and activism.

INDEX

About the Author

Megan Kopp lives with a firefighter and a nurse. It's a family full of critical thinkers. As a writer, Megan's list of questions is always long. When not analyzing and probing for answers, Megan can be found paddling prairie rivers or hiking mountain paths, and thinking about thinking.